PARTNERSHIP UNDERSTANDINGS

by Mike Lawrence

Published by
Devyn Press
Louisville, Kentucky

Cover by Bonnie Baron Pollack

Devyn Press
151 Thierman Lane
Louisville, KY 40207

ISBN 0-910791-08-2

TABLE OF CONTENTS

INTRODUCTION

My ex-partner and present teammate Mike Lawrence is actually a very clever fellow. (I should have paid more attention to his bids.)

His latest Book-of-the-Month-Club entry (he writes them faster than most people can read them) is a rather nifty book dealing with partnership understandings, probably better entitled "Partnership Misunderstandings."

The reason I consider Mike so clever is that this book will sell in pairs rather than singly. (Why didn't I ever think of that?)

This is a book designed for partnerships. If you either have a partner or are thinking of forming a partnership, sprint, don't run to your nearest bookstore, and pick up not one, but two, of these books.

Now once each of you has one of these books safely in hand, you can begin to answer the questions by filling in the little multiple choice boxes with what you think is the right answer in your partnership. For example, in the section that deals with responding to two notrump we have this question:

Opener	Responder	How do you ask	4NT	☐
2NT	3♣	for aces?	4♣	☐
3♡	?		5♣	☐
			Other	☐

Explain _____

Mike never tells you how he plays or what he thinks is the right answer. The reason is that this book is not intended to show you how he plays. It is intended to make sure you and your partner are on the same wave-length.

This book can save you and your partner hours and hours of work. Almost every conceivable practical sequence that causes trouble because of a possible misunderstanding is covered.

How much did I like this book? Well, in payment for this introduction all I want is two copies of the book. The moment they arrive, one goes to my partner, Billy Eisenberg, so we can start filling in the little boxes. Good work, Michael.

—Edwin B. Kantar

NOTRUMP OPENINGS

After a 1NT opening bid

One notrump shows   Range _____ to _____

Variations

If it varies according to vulnerability or seat, specify

	1st or 2nd Seat	3rd or 4th Seat
Vulnerable	_____ to _____	_____ to _____
Not Vulnerable	_____ to _____	_____ to _____

Will you open 1 NT on all hands which fall into your point range? For example, if you play 15 to 17, how many 15's will you open?

100% ☐
75% ☐
50% ☐
Other ☐

Explain _____

Playing 15 to 17, do you open 1 NT on?

      ♠ K862
      ♡ KJ3   Yes ☐
      ◊ KQ   No ☐
      ♣ QJ96

		SPADES	HEARTS
Do you open 1 NT with five hearts or five spades?	Always	☐	☐
	Occasionally	☐	☐
	Never	☐	☐

If you do open 1 NT with a five card major, how good can your suit be?	Very Good	A K J 8 4	☐
	Good	K Q 7 5 3	☐
	Fair	Q J 8 6 2	☐
	Poor	J 7 5 4 3	☐

If you do open 1 NT with a five card major, will you have all side suits stopped?	Yes ☐
	No ☐

If you do open 1 NT with a five card major, does your point count affect your decision? If yes, explain _____   Yes ☐   No ☐

_____

If you do open 1 NT with a five card major, which of these hands would qualify (assuming 15 to 17)?

♠ A Q 10 8 7	♠ Q 10 8 6 4	♠ J 7 5 4 2	♠ K 7
♡ K Q 7	♡ 4 2	♡ K Q 9	♡ K J 9 6 5
◊ 10 5 4	◊ A K J	◊ A J	◊ A Q 10
♣ A J	♣ A Q 10	♣ K Q 8	♣ K 8 5
1NT ☐	1NT ☐	1NT ☐	1NT ☐
1♠ ☐	1♠ ☐	1♠ ☐	1♡ ☐

If you do open 1 NT with a five card major, do you intend to show it or to ignore it?   Show it ☐   Ignore it ☐

1NT	2♣	3♠ shows	5 Spades	☐
3♠			Does not exist	☐
			Other	☐

Explain _____

1NT	2♣	3♠ shows	5 Spades	☐
2♠	3◊		Cue bid for diamonds	☐
3♠			Other	☐

Explain _____

Do you open 1 NT with a   Yes ☐
small doubleton?   No ☐

♠ 8 2	♠ A Q 9 7	♠ A Q 9
♡ A Q 9 7	♡ 8 2	♡ 8 2
◇ K Q J 4	◇ K Q J 4	◇ K Q J 4 2
♣ K J 7	♣ K J 7	♣ K J 7
1NT ☐	1NT ☐	1NT ☐
Other_____	Other_____	Other_____

Stayman

What kind of Stayman   2♣ non forcing   ☐
do you use?   2♣ forcing   ☐
                                 Two-way with
          2♣ non forcing and 2◇ forcing   ☐

If you play Nonforcing 2♣

1NT	2♣	Do you ever answer with anything	Yes ☐
?		other than 2◇, 2♡, or 2♠?	No ☐

                             If yes, explain _____

_____

1NT	2♣	If opener has two four card majors,	2♠ ☐
?		what does he bid?	2♡ ☐
			The better suit ☐
			Other ☐

                     Explain _____

1NT	2♣	2♡ is	Signoff ☐
2◇	2♡		Invitational ☐

               Scrambling from 1 NT.
               It shows a weak hand with
               4♠ + 5♡, 4♠ + 4♡, or 5♠ + 4♡   ☐
                                        Other   ☐

                     Explain _____

1NT	2♣	2♠ is	Signoff ☐
2♡	2♠		Invitational ☐
			Forcing ☐
			Other ☐

                     Explain _____

How do you escape to clubs with a weak hand?	Can't do it	☐
	1NT - 3♣	☐
	1NT - 2♣	
	2x - 3♣	☐
	1NT - 2♠ (Transfer)	☐
	1NT - 2NT (Transfer)	☐
	Other	☐

Explain _____

If you play 2♣ Forcing Stayman

1NT 2♣	Do you ever answer	Yes ☐
?	anything other than	No ☐
	2◇, 2♡, or 2♠	

If yes, explain _____

_____

1NT 2♣	If opener has two	2♠	☐
?	four card majors,	2♡	☐
	what does he bid?	The better suit	☐
		Other	☐

Explain _____

How do you escape to clubs with a weak hand?	Can't do it	☐
	1NT - 3♣	☐
	1NT - 2♣	
	2x - 3♣	☐
	1NT - 2♠ (Transfer)	☐
	1NT - 2NT (Transfer)	☐
	Other	☐

Explain _____

If you play Two-Way Stayman

| 1NT 2♣ | Do you ever answer anything | Yes ☐ |
| ? | other than 2◇, 2♡. or 2♠? | No ☐ |

If yes, explain _____

_____

1NT	2♣		If opener has two	2♠	☐
?			four card majors,	2♡	☐
			what does he bid?	The better suit	☐
				Other	☐

Explain _____

| 1NT | 2♣ | 2♡ is | | Signoff | ☐ |
| 2◊ | 2♡ | | | Invitational | ☐ |

Scrambling from Invitational.
It shows a weak hand with
4♠ + 5♡, 4♠ + 4♡, or 5♠ + 4♡ ☐
Other ☐

Explain _____

1NT	2♣	3♡ is		Forcing	☐
2◊	3♡			Invitational	☐
				Other	☐

Explain _____

1NT	2◊		If opener has two	2♡	☐
?			four card majors,	2♠	☐
			what does he bid?	The better suit	☐
				Other	☐

Explain _____

1NT	2◊	This shows	A good five card suit	☐
3♣ or 3◊			Any five card suit	☐
			Good four card suit	☐
			Other	☐

Explain _____

| 1NT | 2◊ | 3♡ shows | A five card suit | ☐ |
| 3♡ | | | Other | ☐ |

Explain _____

If two clubs is doubled

Does pass by opener deny a major suit?   Yes ☐
                                               No ☐

If opener passes, how good are his clubs? _____

_____

If opener redoubles, how good are his clubs? _____

_____

1NT	Pass	2♣	Dbl	Redouble is	SOS ☐
Pass	Pass	Rdbl			Let's play 2♣
					redoubled ☐

If one notrump is doubled

YOU	LHO	PARTNER		
1NT	Dbl*	2♣		*Penalty double

Is 2♣   Natural ☐
                 Stayman ☐
                 Transfer ☐

YOU	LHO	PARTNER		
1NT	Dbl*	2♣		*A one suited hand

Is 2♣   Natural ☐
                 Stayman ☐
                 Transfer ☐

YOU	LHO	PARTNER		
1NT	Dbl*	Redbl		*Penalty double

Is Redbl   Business ☐
                 SOS ☐
                 Other ☐

Explain _____

YOU	LHO	PARTNER		
1NT	Dbl*	Redbl		* A one suited hand

Is Redbl   Business ☐
                 SOS ☐
                 Other ☐

Explain _____

If the opening notrump bidder doubles without hearing from partner

YOU	LHO	PART.	RHO
1NT	2♠	Pass	Pass	Double is	Takeout ☐
Dbl					Penalty ☐

YOU	LHO	PART.	RHO
1NT	Pass	Pass	2♠	Double is	Takeout ☐
Dbl					Penalty ☐

If you play Jacoby Transfers

1NT	2◇	3♡ is	A maximum with 4 hearts ☐
3♡			Does not exist ☐
			Other ☐

Explain _____

1NT	2◇	2NT is	A maximum with 3 hearts ☐
2NT			Does not exist ☐
			Other ☐

Explain _____

1NT	2◇	These bids	Do not exist ☐
2♠, 3♣, or 3◇			Show five card suits ☐
			Show a maximum and a heart fit ☐
			Other ☐

Explain _____

1NT	2◇	3♣ is	Natural, game forcing ☐
2♡	3♣		Natural, invitational ☐
			Other ☐

Explain _____

1NT	2◇	Can you ask for aces?	Yes ☐
2♡	?		No ☐

Explain _____

I recommend that if you use Jacoby Transfers, you also use Texas. This permits:

1NT	2◇		1NT	4◇	
2◇	4NT	Quantitative	4♡	4NT	Blackwood

If your Jacoby Transfer is doubled

YOU	LHO	PART.	RHO
1NT	Pass	2♡ *	Dbl**

                        * Jacoby for Spades
                        ** Penalty double

If opener passes	He shows two spades	☐
	He is willing to play in 2♡ doubled	☐
	Other	☐

Explain _____

If opener redoubles	He wants to play in 2♡ redoubled	☐
	Other	☐

Explain _____

1NT	2◇	4♣ is	Gerber	☐
2♡	4♣		A club void	☐
			A club singleton	☐
			A five card suit	☐
			Other	☐

Explain _____

How do you get to play 3♣ or 3◇   Explain _____
if responder has a hopeless
hand with a long minor?   _____
_____
_____

If one notrump is doubled

1NT	Dbl*	2◇	* Penalty double		
			Is 2◇	Natural	☐
				Jacoby	☐

1NT	Dbl*	2◇	* A one suited hand		
			Is 2◇	Natural	☐
				Jacoby	☐

If you use Texas Transfers

Do you use normal Texas
  4◊ = Hearts
  4♡ = Spades

        or   Normal Texas ☐
                                           South African
Do you use the South African version?   Texas   ☐
  4♣ = Hearts
  4◊ = Spades

If there is competition, is Texas   Yes ☐
still on?   No ☐

                    If yes, explain when Texas no longer

                    applies _____

                    _____

                    _____

If 1 NT is doubled, Texas is   On ☐
                                                       Off ☐

If you play 1NT - Pass - 3♣/3◊   6 cards with
is invitational, how good is   two of the
your suit?   three top honors ☐
                                       Other   ☐

                    Explain _____

YOU   PARTNER
1NT   3♡   3♡ is   Invitational   ☐
                                        Game force only   ☐
                                        Slammish   ☐
                                        Other   ☐

                    Explain _____

13

YOU	PARTNER			
1NT	3♡	4♡ is	Sign off	☐
3NT	4♡		Slammish	☐

YOU	PARTNER			
1♣	1♡	4♡ is	Sign off	☐
2NT	3♡		Slammish	☐
3NT	4♡			

YOU	PARTNER			
1♣	1♡	4♡ is	Sign off	☐
2NT	4♡		Slammish	☐

Explain the difference between the last two sequences? _____

_____

What do these sequences mean?

YOU	LHO	PARTNER			
1NT	2♡	3♣/3◇	3♣/3◇ is	Forcing	☐
				Invitational	☐
				Competitive only	☐
				Other	☐

Explain _____

YOU	LHO	PARTNER			
1NT	2♣	3♡	3♡ is	Forcing	☐
				Invitational	☐
				Competitive only	☐
				Other	☐

Explain _____

After a 2NT opening bid

What is your 2NT range? _____ to _____

Can you have a five card major?
Yes ☐
No ☐

Can you have a small doubleton?
Yes ☐
No ☐

In response to Stayman, what
does opener bid with two
four card majors?

3♡ ☐
3♠ ☐
The better suit ☐
Other ☐

Explain _____

QUESTIONS

2NT 3♣	How do you ask	4NT ☐
3♡	for aces?	4♣ ☐
		5♣ ☐
		Other ☐

Explain _____

| 2NT 3♣ | 4NT is | Quantitative ☐ |
| 3♡ 4NT | | For aces ☐ |

2NT 3♣	4♣ is	A suit ☐
3♡ 4♣		For aces ☐
		Cue bid ☐

2NT 3♣	5♣ is	A suit ☐
3♡ 5♣		For aces ☐
		Other ☐

If you use Jacoby Transfers over 2 NT

(Recommend that if you use Jacoby, you also use Texas.)

What do these sequences mean?

2NT 3◇	4♡ is	Excellent hand ☐
4♡		for hearts
		Other ☐

Explain _____

2NT	3◇	3♠ is	Cue bid for hearts	☐
3♠			Five spades and bad hearts	☐
			Other	☐

Explain _____

| 2NT | 3◇ | 3NT is | Excellent hand for hearts, 3 card support | ☐ |
| | | | Terrible hand for hearts. Prefer notrump | ☐ |

2NT	3◇	4♣ is	Singleton club	☐
3♡	4♣		Club suit	☐
			Cue bid for hearts	☐
			Gerber	☐
			Other	☐

Explain _____

| 2NT | 3◇ | 4NT is | Quantitative | ☐ |
| 3♡ | 4NT | | For aces | ☐ |

Explain any other understandings you have regarding Jacoby transfers.

_____

_____

_____

If you play Texas over 2 NT

Which version do you play?   Normal   ☐
                                     South African   ☐

If you use natural responses

YOU	PARTNER		
2NT	3♡ *	* Natural	4♡ is sign off ☐
3NT	4♡		Slammish ☐

YOU	PARTNER		
2NT	4♡ *	* Natural	4♡ is sign off ☐
			Slammish ☐

What is the difference between the last two sequences? _____

_____

_____

3 NT Openings

An opening 3NT is

Gambling	☐
ACOL	☐
25-27 HCP	☐
Other	☐

Explain _____

If 3 NT is gambling, how
many outside stoppers can
you have? Check all
boxes that apply.

2 stoppers	☐
1½ stoppers	☐
1 stopper	☐
½ stopper	☐
0 stopper	☐

Can you have a singleton?

Yes ☐
No ☐

If your gambling 3NT is doubled,
is the opener supposed to run
out or should he leave that
decision to partner?

Opener ☐
Responder ☐

If 3NT is ACOL

How many side stoppers
are required? Check appropriate
boxes.

2½ stoppers	☐
2 stoppers	☐
1½ stoppers	☐
1 stopper	☐

Can opener have a singleton?

Yes ☐
No ☐

Is a 4♣ response

For aces ☐
To escape ☐

If 3NT is a big balanced hand

How do you ask for a major?

4♣ ☐
4◇ ☐
Can't ☐

How do you ask for aces?

4♣ ☐
4◇ ☐
4NT ☐
5♣ ☐

MAJOR SUIT OPENINGS

If you play 4-card majors

What you do open with (generally speaking)?

4 Spades + 4 Hearts	1 Spade	☐
	1 Heart	☐
4 Spades + 5 Hearts	1 Spade	☐
	1 Heart	☐
	Flannery 2 Diamonds	☐
4 Hearts + 5 Diamonds	1 Heart	☐
	1 Diamond	☐
4 Diamonds + 4 Clubs	1 Diamond	☐
	1 Club	☐
4 Diamonds + 5 Clubs	1 Diamond	☐
	1 Club	☐
3 Diamonds + 3 Clubs	1 Diamond	☐
(Assuming no biddable major)	1 Club	☐
5 Spades + 5 Clubs	1 Spade	☐
	1 Club	☐

If partner opens one diamond, would you respond 1 ♡ on

♡ 9 7 6 2	Yes	☐
	No	☐
♡ K 10 7 3	Yes	☐
	No	☐
♡ 6 5 4 2	Yes	☐
	No	☐

If partner opens one diamond, would you ever respond 1 ♡ with only three hearts?

Yes ☐
No ☐

Does a two over one promise another bid?

i.e. 1♠ 2♣
      2♠

Yes ☐
No ☐

Explain _____

What do these sequences show?

1♠　2♣　　　Range for 2NT is _____ to _____
2NT　　　　It is forcing　　　　　　　　☐
　　　　　　　　non forcing　　　　　　☐

1♠　2♣　　　Range for 3NT is _____ to _____
3NT　　　　Range for 3♣ is _____ to _____

1♠　2♣　　　3♣ is forcing　　　　　　　☐
3♣　　　　　　　non forcing　　　　　☐

If you play five card majors

What do you open with (generally speaking)?

4 Diamonds + 4 Clubs	1 Diamond	☐
	1 Club	☐
4 Diamonds + 5 Clubs	1 Diamond	☐
	1 Club	☐
3 Diamonds + 3 Clubs	1 Diamond	☐
	1 Club	☐
5 Spades + 5 Clubs	1 Spade	☐
	1 Club	☐
	Depends on the hand	☐

Explain _____

Does a two over one response guarantee another bid?	Yes	☐
	No	☐
Is a two over one response	100% game forcing	☐
	90% game forcing	☐
	Other	☐

Explain _____

_____

_____

If a two over one response is not 100% game forcing, which of these sequences can be passed by opener? If necessary, explain responder's last bid.

			Forcing	☐
1♠	2♣		Not Forcing	☐
2♠	3♣			
		Explain _____		

			Forcing	☐
1♠	2♣		Not Forcing	☐
2◇	3♣			
		Explain _____		

			Forcing	☐
1♠	2♣		Not Forcing	☐
2NT	3♣			
		Explain _____		

			Forcing	☐
1♡	2◇		Not Forcing	☐
2♠	3◇			
		Explain _____		

			Forcing	☐
1♠	2♣		Not Forcing	☐
2♡	2♠			
		Explain _____		

			Forcing	☐
1♠	2♣		Not Forcing	☐
2♠	3♣			
		Explain _____		

			Forcing	☐
1◇	2♣		Not Forcing	☐
2◇	2NT			
		Explain _____		

Regardless of whether you play four or five card majors

If you play limit raises

How many trump do you promise	Three	☐
	Four	☐
Do you promise a singleton	Yes	☐
	No	☐

If you play Drury

Is Drury on after

Pass Pass 1♡ 1♠	Is 2♣ Drury?	Yes	☐
2♣		No	☐

Is Drury on after

Pass Pass 1♡ Dbl	Is 2♣ Drury?	Yes	☐
2♣		No	☐

Is Drury on after

Pass Pass Pass 1♡	Is 2♣ Drury?	Yes	☐
1NT* 2♣		No	☐

* Unusual because it is by a passed hand.

After

      Pass Pass 1♡ Pass
      2♣ ?

How does opener show a weak hand?	Two hearts	☐
	Two diamonds	☐
Does the Drury response absolutely promise three trump or can responder do it with two?	Promises three	☐
	No promise	☐

QUESTIONS

1. Pass Pass 1♡   Pass   Opener's rebids show
   2♣   Pass 2♠
                                              1 2 3
2. Pass Pass 1♡   Pass   A slammish hand
   2♣   Pass 3♣   with a second suit   □ □ □
3. Pass Pass 1♡   Pass   Just an opening bid
   2♣   Pass 3◇   with a second suit   □ □ □

                            A singleton with
                              a good hand   □ □ □
                            Other   □ □ □

                    Explain _____

                    _____

4. Pass Pass 1♡   Pass   Opener's rebids show
   2♣   Pass 3♠
                                              4 5 6
5. Pass Pass 1♡   Pass   A slammish hand
   2♣   Pass 4♣   with a void   □ □ □
6. Pass Pass 1♡   Pass   A slammish hand
   2♣   Pass 4◇   with a singleton   □ □ □

                            A slammish hand with
                              either a void or a
                              singleton   □ □ □
                            A slammish hand
                              with a second suit □ □ □
                            Other   □ □ □

                    Explain _____

What does this mean?

Pass Pass 1♡ Pass   3♡ is   Slammish □
2♣   Pass 3♡   Other   □

                    Explain _____

Pass Pass 1♡ Pass   4♡ is   Slammish □
2♣   Pass 4♡   Sign off □
                                           Other   □

                    Explain _____

24

Game tries after a major raise

LHO	PART.
1♠	2♠
3♣	

What kind of holding does 3♣ show? Check appropriate boxes.

A K Q 9	☐
A Q 9 7	☐
A 10 7 5	☐
K J 5 2	☐
K 7 6 5	☐
Q 7 5 4	☐
J 10 4 3	☐
10 6 3 2	☐
9 4 3 2	☐
A singleton	☐
Other	☐

Explain _____

For example:

YOU	PART.
1♠	2♠
?	

If you choose to make a game try, which would it be?

♠ A J 9 7 6	3♣	☐
♡ 2	3◇	☐
◇ Q 8 6	3♡	☐
♣ A K J 5	3♠	☐
	2NT	☐

What kind of game tries do you play after a major raise?

Short suit	☐
Long suit	☐
Help suit	☐
Other	☐

Explain _____

_____

TWO BIDS

After a strong Two Club opening

is 2♣   Game Force ☐
                                                          Other   ☐

                Explain _____

                               _____

What does partner need to respond
      2♡ or 2♠

                Explain _____

                               _____

      3♣ or 3♢

                Explain _____

                               _____

      2NT

	Does not exist	☐
Balanced ____ to ____ HCP		☐
	Other	☐

                Explain _____

      3NT

	Does not exist	☐
Balanced ____ to ____ HCP		☐
	Other	☐

                Explain _____

After   2♣   2♢
           2♡   ?

What is responder's second negative?   Two spades ☐
                                           Two notrump ☐
                                           Three clubs ☐
                                           None ☐

After   2♣   2♢
           3♢   ?

Do you have a second negative?   Yes ☐
                                             No   ☐

                Explain _____

If an opponent overcalls,
what does double mean?

			Dbl =	Penalty	☐
				Negative	☐
				Positive	☐
2♣	2♠	Dbl		Other	☐

Explain _____

If an opponent overcalls, do partner's
bids mean the same as if there were
no overcall?

The same	☐
Same values, but	
the suit may	
be shaded	☐
Less values	☐
More values	☐
Other	☐

Explain _____

♠ K 8 4	PART.	RHO	YOU	Two diamonds ☐
♡ 9 7	2♣	Pass	?	Three clubs ☐
◇ K 5 3				Other ☐
♣ Q 10 9 6 3				

Explain _____

♠ K 8 4	PART.	RHO	YOU	Pass ☐
♡ 9 7	2♣	2♡	?	Double ☐
◇ K 5 3				Three clubs ☐
♣ Q 10 9 6 3				Other ☐

Explain _____

If you play Flannery

2◇   Pass 2NT   Game Forcing   ☐
                                    Forcing to 3♡ or 3♠ ☐
                                    Other   ☐

♠ K Q 7 2   YOU
♡ A Q J 8 5   2◇   Pass 2NT Pass
◇ Q 8 7
♣ 2

                  Opener rebids —   3◇ showing
                                       three   ☐
                                      3♣ showing
                                      a singleton ☐

2◇   Pass. 3♡ or 3♣   Forcing   ☐
                                    Invitational ☐
                                    Other   ☐

2◇   Pass 3◇   Forcing   ☐
                                    Invitational ☐
                                    Other   ☐

                      Explain _____

2◇   Pass 3♣   Forcing   ☐
                                    Invitational ☐
                                    Sign off   ☐
                                    Other   ☐

                      Explain _____

Do you have any special treatment regarding Flannery such as:

   Can you have a void?
   Can you have 4 spades + 6 hearts?

                      Explain _____

                                 _____

                                 _____

                                 _____

If you play weak two bids

What is your range?

	1st & 2nd Seat	3rd Seat	4th Seat
Not vulnerable	___ to ___	___ to ___	___ to ___
Vulnerable	___ to ___	___ to ___	___ to ___

In first or second seat

What is your worst suit?

Explain _____

_____

Can you have a void?

Yes ☐
Unlikely ☐
No ☐

Can you have a side four card major?

Yes ☐
Unlikely ☐
No ☐

Can you have two aces?

Yes ☐
Unlikely ☐
No ☐

Would you describe your
weak twos as

Classical ☐
You like to mix it
   up a little ☐
You like to push the
   opponents around ☐
Anything goes ☐

In third seat

Can you have a five card suit?

Yes ☐
Likely ☐
Unlikely ☐
No ☐

How do your third seat weak twos
compare to your first seat two bids?

Same ☐
A bit more
   aggressive ☐
A lot more
   aggressive ☐

In fourth seat

Your weak twos are

Solid ten to
twelve point
hand with
good six
card suit ☐
Other ☐

Explain _____

If you play Ogust, are you sure
you know the responses?

Yes ☐
No ☐

YOU	LHO	PART.	RHO		
2♠	Pass	2NT	Pass	Can opener bid	Yes ☐
3◇ *	Pass	3♠	Pass	again?	No ☐
?					

*Feature with extra values

After 2♠ by you and 2NT by partner what do the following
mean?

3♠ Outside feature ☐
Other ☐

Explain _____

3◇ Outside feature ☐
Other ☐

Explain _____

3♡ Outside feature ☐
Other ☐

Explain _____

3♠ Minimum with no
outside feature ☐
Other ☐

Explain _____

3NT Solid suit ☐
Other ☐

Explain _____

DOUBLES

If you play negative doubles

| 1♣ | 1♡ | Dbl | Double shows | Three spades ☐ |
| | | | | Four spades ☐ |

| 1♣ | 1♢ | Dbl | Double promises four | Yes ☐ |
| | | | cards in both majors | No ☐ |

| 1♣ | 1♠ | Dbl | | |

Does double also promise diamond support?   Yes ☐
                                            No ☐

Explain _____

| PART. | RHO | YOU |
| 1♣ | 1♡ | ? |

What would you do with each of these hands?

♠ Q 10 7
♡ 9 6 5
♢ K J 10 8 7
♣ Q 2

Pass	☐
Dbl	☐
Other	☐

Explain _____

♠ Q 9 6 4 2
♡ 8
♢ A 10 8 6 4
♣ K 9

One spade	☐
Dbl	☐
Other	☐

Explain _____

♠ K Q 10 7
♡ 8 6 5
♢ 8 3
♣ Q 10 4 3

Pass	☐
Dbl	☐
One spade	☐
Other	☐

Explain _____

♠ J 8 6 5
♡ A 2
♢ A K J 9 3
♣ Q 10

One spade	☐
Two diamonds	☐
Two hearts	☐
Dbl	☐
Other	☐

Explain _____

PART.	RHO	YOU	What would you do with each of
1♣	1♠	?	these hands?

♠ K 8 7
♡ Q 10 8 3
◊ 4 2
♣ K 7 5 3

INT	☐
Dbl	☐
2 clubs	☐
Pass	☐
Other	☐

Explain _____

♠ J 9 7
♡ Q J 9 6 5
◊ K 4 2
♣ Q 3

Pass	☐
2 hearts	☐
Dbl	☐
Other	☐

Explain _____

♠ 8 6 2
♡ A Q 5
◊ Q 10 8 6 4
♣ J 3

Dbl	☐
2 diamonds	☐
Pass	☐
Other	☐

Explain _____

♠ K 5
♡ A K 10 6 4
◊ A 10 7 3 2
♣ 9

Dbl	☐
2 hearts	☐
2 diamonds	☐
2 spades	☐
Other	☐

Explain _____

If you play responsive doubles

Do you play them after partner makes a takeout double?	Yes ☐	No ☐
Do you play them after partner overcalls?	Yes ☐	No ☐
Do you play them if partner makes a weak jump overcall?	Yes ☐	No ☐

Do you play them after three-suited auctions? For example:

LHO	PART.	RHO	YOU
1♣	1♢	1♠	?

Is a double by you responsive?   Yes ☐
      No ☐

If you play Maximal game try doubles

Do you use them only when the opponents have a fit, or all the time?

For example:

1♠	2♡	2♠	3♡	They have a fit.	Dbl is	Responsive ☐ Penalty ☐
Dbl						
1♠	Dbl	2♠	3♡	They have a fit.	Dbl is	Responsive ☐ Penalty ☐
Dbl						
1♠	Pass	2♠	3♡	No fit.	Dbl is	Responsive ☐ Penalty ☐
Dbl						

COMPETITIVE BIDDING

When you overcall 1NT

What is your range? _____ to _____

When you overcall 1NT, what is your response structure? (Do you play 2♣ or a cue bid as Stayman? Do you play transfers?)

Explain _____

_____

_____

_____

| 1♣ | Pass | 1♡ | 1NT | 1 NT is | A strong NT ☐ |
| | | | | | Unusual ☐ |

When you overcall

How aggressive are you at the one level? Does the vulnerability make any difference?

Explain _____

_____

How aggressive are you at the two level? Does the vulnerability make any difference?

Explain _____

_____

Can you ever have a four card suit?

Explain _____

_____

Is a new suit by responder **ever** forcing?

Explain _____

_____

A jump shift after an overcall is

1♣	1♡	Pass	2♠	Forcing ☐
		or		Invitational ☐
1♣	1♡	Pass	3◇	Pre-emptive ☐
				Depends on the
				opponents'
				bidding ☐
				Other ☐

Explain _____

What does a cue bid mean in response to an overcall?

1◇   1♠   Pass   2◇

Explain _____

_____

What does a jump cue bid mean?

1♣   1♡   Pass   3♣

Explain _____

1♡   2♣   Pass   3♡

Explain _____

If you use weak jump overcalls

How pushy do you get?
Give examples of the best and worst hands you might have.

RHO   YOU
1♣   2♠

You are	The best hand you can have.	The worst hand you can have.
Vul. vs. Vul.		
Vul. vs. Not Vul.		
No One Vul.		
Not Vul. vs Vul.		

35

RHO   YOU
1♠   3♣

	The best hand you can have.	The worst hand you can have.
Vul. vs Vul.		
Vul. vs. Not Vul.		
Not Vul. vs. Vul.		
No One Vul.		

Can you have a five card suit?   Frequently ☐
                                        Seldom ☐
                                        No ☐

What is your system   New suit forcing ☐
of responses?   Lead directing ☐
                                        Non forcing ☐
                                        Other ☐

Explain _____

RHO   YOU   LHO   PART.
1♣   2♦   Pass   2NT

2 NT is

Explain _____

_____

36

After an opponent's takeout double

What does a jump shift to the two level look like?
1♣ Dbl 2♦

Preemptive ☐
Like a weak two ☐
Forcing ☐
Other ☐

                           Explain _____

What does a jump shift to the three level look like?
1♠ Dbl 3♣

Preemptive ☐
Like a weak two ☐
Forcing ☐
Other ☐

                           Explain _____

If 2NT is a limit raise, does it show three or four trump?

Three ☐
Four ☐

Do you use the 2NT limit raise the same way in the minors as in the majors?

Yes ☐
No ☐
Don't use ☐
Other ☐

                           Explain _____

AFTER THE OPPONENTS OPEN

When the opponents open a weak two

A 2NT overcall is

12 to 15	☐
15 to 19	☐
Unusual	☐
Other	☐

Explain _____

What is your response structure?

Explain _____

A cue bid is

The majors if the opening bid was 2◇	☐
Unusual if the opening bid was 2♡ or 2♠	☐
Asking for a stopper for 3NT	☐
High-low cue bid	☐
A huge two-suited hand	☐
A huge three-suited hand	☐
Other	☐

Explain _____

_____

When the opponents open with a three bid

A cue bid is   The majors if the opening
                                       bid was 3♣ or 3◇   ☐

                                   The minors if the opening
                                       bid was 3♡ or 3♠   ☐

                                   A huge unspecified two
                                       suiter   ☐

                                   Other   ☐

                Explain _____

What is your response structure if partner overcalls with a
3NT bid?

                Explain _____

When the opponents open 4♣, 4♦, or 4♡

Is double takeout?   Yes ☐
                                           No ☐

When the opponents open 4♠

Is double takeout or business?   Penalty ☐
                                       Takeout ☐

What is 4NT?   Minors ☐
                                       Three suits ☐
                                       An unknown
                                          two suiter ☐
                                       Other   ☐

                Explain _____

If you play Michaels or the unusual notrump

Do you show   Any point range   ☐
                                 Either 9 to 12 or 16 +   ☐
                                   Other   ☐

                     Explain _____

Over one club, do you bid Michaels on any of these hands?
        No one vulnerable.   Both Vulnerable.

1♣   ?

♠ K 10 8 6 5	Yes ☐		Yes ☐	
♡ Q J 8 4 2	No ☐		No ☐	
◊ K 3				
♣ 7				
♠ A J 10 8 7	Yes ☐		Yes ☐	
♡ K Q 10 9 5	No ☐		No ☐	
◊ 3				
♣ K 8				
♠ A K J 7 2	Yes ☐		Yes ☐	
♡ A Q 10 9 5	No ☐		No ☐	
◊ K 5				
♣ J				
♠ K Q 9 7 5	Yes ☐		Yes ☐	
♡ A Q J 2	No ☐		No ☐	
◊ 8				
♣ 9 7 5				
♠ A Q J 2	Yes ☐		Yes ☐	
♡ K Q 9 7 5	No ☐		No ☐	
◊ 3				
♣ 8 6 4				

Over one spade, would you bid any unusual 2NT with any of these? No one vulnerable.   Both vulnerable.

♠ 2   Yes ☐   Yes ☐
♡ 8 5   No ☐   No ☐
◊ K 10 8 7 5
♣ A 10 7 4 2

♠ K 3   Yes ☐   Yes ☐
♡ 2   No ☐   No ☐
◊ A J 9 8 7
♣ K Q 10 7 4

♠ A Q   Yes ☐   Yes ☐
♡ 2   No ☐   No ☐
◊ K Q J 9 7
♣ A Q 10 6 4

♠ J 5 4   Yes ☐   Yes ☐
♡ 8   No ☐   No ☐
◊ A Q 10 8
♣ K Q 10 6 4

Do you have any agreements on Michaels or unusual notrump?

Explain _____

_____

_____

If the opponents bid two suits, what does a cue bid mean?

1♣ Pass 1♠ 2♣   Natural ☐
                                           Takeout ☐
                                           Other   ☐

Explain _____

1♣ Pass 1♠ 2♠   Natural ☐
                                           Takeout ☐
                                           Other   ☐

Explain _____

41

YOUR BIDDING STYLE

In general, are your opening bids

Aggressive ☐
Normal ☐
Ultra sound ☐

	N.V.	Vul.
How many balanced twelve counts do you open? 100%	☐	☐
75%	☐	☐
50%	☐	☐
Other	_____	

In first seat, would you open these hands?

		Not				Not
	Vul.	Vul.			Vul.	Vul.
♠ K8765 ♡ AJ974 ◇ Q9 ♣ 5	Yes ☐ No ☐	☐ ☐	♠ A62 ♡ 654 ◇ 9532 ♣ AK8	Yes ☐ No ☐	☐ ☐
♠ 842 ♡ KQ ◇ QJ2 ♣ KQ632	Yes ☐ No ☐	☐ ☐	♠ K1085 ♡ AJ54 ◇ 863 ♣ AJ	Yes ☐ No ☐	☐ ☐
♠ AQ2 ♡ KJ5 ◇ 1094 ♣ Q1097	Yes ☐ No ☐	☐ ☐	♠ A1082 ♡ KJ53 ◇ 4 ♣ K974	Yes ☐ No ☐	☐ ☐

Are you apt to psyche in third seat?

Yes ☐
No ☐

If yes, what would it look like?

_____

_____

Do you use the principle of fast or slow arrival?

1♠	Pass	2♣	Pass	Which is stronger?	3♠	☐
2◇	Pass	?			4♠	☐

Reason _____

_____

Would you raise partner's one level response with three trump or do you require four?

Three ☐
Four ☐

Do you raise with three trump in competition?

Yes ☐
No ☐

After the given sequence, would you raise with the example hand?

No competition   In competition

YOU		PART.		YOU		PART.	
1◇	Pass	1♡	Pass	1◇	Pass	1♡	1♠
?							

♠ 82	2♡ ☐		2♡ ☐
♡ KJ7	Other ___		Other ___
◇ AQJ86			
♣ K95			

♠ 7	2♡ ☐		2♡ ☐
♡ J95	Other ___		Other ___
◇ KQ1087			
♣ AQ75			

♠ 864	2♡ ☐		2♡ ☐
♡ AQ2	Other ___		Other ___
◇ AKJ3			
♣ 952			

♠ A94	2♡ ☐		2♡ ☐
♡ KJ8	Other ___		Other ___
◇ J865			
♣ KQ2			

♠ K975	2♡ ☐		2♡ ☐
♡ AJ4	Other ___		Other ___
◇ KQ75			
♣ 92			

Secondary jumps

How do you play secondary jumps?

    Forcing ☐
    Invitational ☐
    Depends on the
        sequence ☐

Identify these sequences.

1♣	Pass	1♡	Pass		Forcing	☐
1♠	Pass	3♣			Invitational	☐
1♣	Pass	1♡	Pass		Forcing	☐
1♠	Pass	3♡			Invitational	☐
1♣	Pass	1♡	Pass		Forcing	☐
1♠	Pass	3♠			Invitational	☐
1♣	Pass	1♡	Pass		Forcing	☐
1♠	Pass	2NT			Invitational	☐
1♣	Pass	1◇	Pass		Forcing	☐
1♠	Pass	3♣			Invitational	☐
1♣	Pass	1♡	Pass		Forcing	☐
1NT	Pass	3♣			Invitational	☐
1♣	Pass	1♡	Pass		Forcing	☐
1NT	Pass	3♡			Invitational	☐
1♣	Pass	1♠	Pass		Forcing	☐
1NT	Pass	3◇			Invitational	☐
					Weak	☐

If you play fourth suit forcing

1♣	Pass	1♡	Pass	Is 2◇	Game forcing	☐
1♠	Pass	2◇			Forcing to 2NT	☐
					One round force only	☐
					Other	☐

Explain _____

Reverses

1♣	Pass	1♠	Pass	Is 2♡	Game forcing	☐
2♡					One round force only	☐
					Other	☐

Explain _____

1♣	Pass	1♠	Pass	Explain	2♡	_____
2◇	Pass	?			2♠	_____
					2NT	_____
					3♣	_____
					3◇	_____
					3NT	_____

Do you have any general rules concerning reverses?

_____

_____

_____

Partner opens, RHO overcalls

What does a cue bid mean?

1♡	2♣	3♣	3♣ is	Game forcing raise	☐
				Limit raise	☐
				Looking for NT	☐
				Other	☐

Explain _____

1♣	1♡	2♡	2♡ is	Game forcing raise	☐
				Limit raise	☐
				Looking for NT	☐
				Ohter	☐

Explain _____

What does a jump cue bid mean?

1♣	1♡	3♡	3♡ is	Forcing club raise	
				with a stiff heart	☐
				Asking bid	☐
				Other	☐

Explain _____

1♡	2◇	4◇	4◇ is	Forcing heart raise with	
				a stiff diamond	☐
				Forcing heart raise with	
				a diamond void	☐
				Forcing heart raise with	
				either a stiff or a void	
				in diamonds	☐
				Other	☐

Explain _____

BALANCING

1♠	Pass	Pass	1NT	1NT = _____ to _____
1♡	Pass	Pass	1NT	1NT = _____ to _____
1◇	Pass	Pass	1NT	1NT = _____ to _____
1♣	Pass	Pass	1NT	1NT = _____ to _____

Do you promise a stopper in opener's suit?   Yes ☐
                                                    No ☐

Explain _____

What is your response structure over a balancing 1NT bid?

_____

1♡	Pass	Pass	2NT	2NT is	19 to 21 balanced points with a heart stopper ☐
					Unusual ☐
					Other ☐

Explain _____

1♣	Pass	Pass	2NT	2NT is	19 to 21 balanced points with a club stopper ☐
					Unusual (lower two suits) ☐
					Other ☐

Explain _____

1♣	Pass	Pass	2♣	2♣ is	Michaels ☐
					Strong one suiter ☐
					Strong two suiter ☐
					Any strong hand ☐
					Asking for a club stopper ☐
					Other ☐

Explain _____

LHO

| 1♡ | Pass | Pass | 2♡ | 2♡ = | _____ |

RHO

| 1♡ | Pass | 1NT | Pass | Dbl = | Takeout | ☐ |
| Pass | Dbl | | | | Penalty | ☐ |

LHO

| 1◇ | Pass | 1♠ | Pass | Dbl = | Takeout | ☐ |
| 1NT | Pass | Pass | Dbl | | Penalty | ☐ |

LHO

| 1◇ | Pass | 1♠ | Pass | 2♣ = | Natural | ☐ |
| 1NT | Pass | Pass | 2♣ | | Takeout over dead notrump | ☐ |

LHO

1♣	Pass	Pass	2♣	2♣ =	Strong	☐
					Intermediate	☐
					Weak	☐

RHO

1◇	Pass	1♠	Pass	Dbl =	Penalty	☐
2♣	Pass	2◇	Pass		Takeout	☐
Pass	Dbl					

LHO

| 1NT | Pass | Pass | Dbl | If 1NT = 15 to 17, |

Double = _____ to _____

If 1NT = 12 to 14,

Double = _____ to _____

ODD DOUBLES

RHO

| 1♣ | Pass | 1♠ | Pass | | Dbl = | Takeout | ☐ |
| 2♣ | Dbl | | | | | Penalty | ☐ |

RHO

| 1♣ | Pass | 1NT | Pass | | Dbl = | Takout | ☐ |
| 2♣ | Dbl | | | | | Penalty | ☐ |

| 1♠ | Pass | Pass | Dbl | When the passer is over the |
| Redbl | Pass | | | spade bidder, does his pass mean |

We're going to beat 1♠ ☐
I don't know what to do ☐

JUMP SHIFTS

If you play strong jump shifts

Do you always require 19 or more points?   Yes ☐
                                                No ☐

What is the least you could have for a jump shift?

Explain _____

_____

After 1♣ from partner, would you jump shift with

1♠   Pass ?   Do you have any
                                       system agreements?

♠ A Q J 8 7   Yes ☐
♡ —   No ☐   Explain _____
♢ 8 6 5
♣ K 9 6 4 2

♠ A Q 10 6 3 2   Yes ☐
♡ A K 7   No ☐   Explain _____
♢ 6 4
♣ A Q

♠ A K Q 10 8 6 4 2   Yes ☐
♡ K 3   No ☐   Explain _____
♢ 8 5
♣ 3

♠ A K Q J 8 6 3 2   Yes ☐
♡ A 3   No ☐   Explain _____
♢ K 5
♣ 4

♠ K Q J 7 6 5   Yes ☐
♡ A Q 2   No ☐   Explain _____
♢ A J
♣ Q 4

♠ A Q J 6 4 2   Yes ☐
♡ A K J 8 5   No ☐   Explain _____
♢ K 2
♣ —

♠ A K J 4 2   Yes ☐
♡ 3   No ☐ Explain _____
◇ K 4 3
♣ K J 4 3

If you are a passed hand

A jump shift shows

A maximum original Pass	☐
A good suit with a fit for partner	☐
A good suit with a fit for partner and a singleton	☐
A singleton plus trump support	☐
A long suit and a weak hand	☐
Other	☐

Explain _____

DEFENDING AGAINST VARIOUS CONVENTIONS

Against 1♣ forcing

Do you use

Double shows the majors ☐
1NT shows the minors ☐
Other ☐

Explain _____

After

1♣   Pass   1◇ (negative)   ?

Double shows the majors ☐
1NT shows the minors ☐
Other ☐

Explain _____

After

1♣   Pass   1♡ (natural)   ?

Double is takeout with
     shortness in hearts ☐
Other ☐

Explain _____

If you pass first and bid later,
you are showing

A very good hand ☐
Just being a
     nuisance ☐

1♣   Pass   1◇   Pass
1♡   Pass   2♡   2♣

Against 2♣ forcing

Double shows

Clubs only ☐
Other ☐

Explain _____

If you overcall, do you have a decent   Decent suit ☐
suit or are you trying to be obstructive?   Obstructive ☐

Not Vulnerable vs. Vulnerable

2♣   ?

♠ K Q J 8 7	2♠	☐
♡ 4 2	Pass	☐
◇ K 7 5	Other	☐
♣ 8 6 2		

♠ K 10 9 7 5 2	2♠	☐
♡ —	3♠	☐
◇ J 7 6 4	Pass	☐
♣ 8 5 3	Other	☐

If they open Flannery

There are a variety of defenses you can use against Flannery.
One possible defense is this:

2◇   ?   Double = Minors
                                2♡ = Takeout double
                                2♠ = Natural
                                2NT = 15 to 19 balanced with
                                      the majors stopped.
                                3♣ or 3◇ = Natural

Do you use   As above ☐
                                               Nothing ☐
                                               Other ☐

Explain _____

_____

If they use Drury

Pass	Pass	1♠	Pass	Double = Clubs ☐
2♣ *	Dbl			Takeout double
*Drury				of spades ☐
				Other ☐

Explain _____

_____

If they use Landy

1NT   2♣   ?

Double shows	Clubs	☐
	Scattered high cards	☐
2♡ or 2♠ shows	Natural	☐
	A stopper with values for a raise to 2NT (or more)	☐
		☐
	Other	☐

Explain _____

3♡ or 3♠ are	Natural	☐
	A singleton with a good hand	☐
	Other	☐

Explain _____

If they use Michaels

1♣   2♣   ?

Double =	Clubs	☐
	Scattered values	☐
2♢	Forcing	☐
	Not forcing	☐
2♡ or 2♠	Natural	☐
	A stopper with values for 2NT (or more)	☐
	Other	☐

Explain_____

3♡ or 3♠	Natural	☐
	Club raise with a singleton	☐
	Other	☐

Explain _____

If they use the unusual notrump

There are a number of things you can do. One of them is called "Unusual vs Unusual." It has many variations. Here is one variation; there are half a dozen more.

PARTNER   RHO
1♡ or 1♠   2NT   ?

3♣ = A limit raise

3◇ = Forcing in the unbid major

3 of partner's suit is a raise with 7 to 9 points.

3 of the other major is natural and nonforcing. It shows about ten points.

3NT is a balanced game forcing raise.

4♣, 4◇ are singletons with support for partner and game values.

Double is a fair hand hoping to penalize the opponents.

Do you use unusual vs unusual?

Yes ☐
No ☐
Other ☐

Explain _____

54

SLAM BIDDING

If you play the grand slam force (GSF)

1♠	3♠		Bid seven with two of
5NT			the top three honors ☐
			Other ☐

Explain _____

When do you use Gerber?

Explain _____

_____

_____

What variety of Blackwood do you use?

	Normal	☐
	Key Card	☐
	Roman Key Card	☐
	Other	☐

Explain _____

_____

What are your responses to Blackwood if you have a void suit?

Explain _____

_____

_____

_____

_____

| Are you required to show your void, or | Must show ☐ |
| can you exercise judgment? | Judgment ☐ |

OPENING LEADS

When you lead from 3 small cards (852) what do you tend to lead in the following situations?

	High (8)	Middle (5)	Low (2)
vs. NT			
Unbid suit	☐	☐	☐
Partner bid suit, you raised	☐	☐	☐
Partner bid suit, you didn't raise	☐	☐	☐
You LHO has bid the suit	☐	☐	☐
vs. a suit contract			
Unbid suit	☐	☐	☐
Partner bid suit, you raised	☐	☐	☐
Partner bid suit, you didn't raise	☐	☐	☐
You LHO has bid the suit	☐	☐	☐

When you lead from 4 or 5 small cards what do you tend to lead?

vs. NT _____

_____

vs. a suit contract _____

_____

If you lead a low card on opening lead do you tend to promise an honor?	Yes	☐	
	No	☐	

Explain _____

_____

If yes, does a 10 count as an honor?	Yes	☐
	No	☐

How often do you underlead aces on opening lead vs. a suit contract?	Frequently	☐
	Occasionally	☐
	Never	☐

OTHER POINTS TO DISCUSS

OTHER POINTS TO DISCUSS

If you have any suggestions for the next edition of this book, the publisher would welcome them.

THE BEST OF DEVYN PRESS
Newly Published Bridge Books

Bridge Conventions Complete
by Amalya Kearse
$17.95

An undated and expanded edition (over 800 pages) of the reference book no duplicate player can afford to be without. The reviews say it all:

"At last! A book with both use and appeal for expert or novice plus everybody in between. Every partnership will find material they will wish to add to their present system. Not only are all the conventions in use anywhere today clearly and aptly described, but Kearse criticizes various treatments regarding potential flaws and how they can be circumvented.

"Do yourself a favor and add this book to your shelf even if you don't enjoy most bridge books. This book is a treat as well as a classic."
—ACBL BULLETIN

"A must for duplicate fans, this is a comprehensive, well-written guide through the maze of systems and conventions. This should be particularly useful to those who don't want to be taken off guard by an unfamiliar convention, because previously it would have been necessary to amass several references to obtain all the information presented."
—BRIDGE WORLD MAGAZINE

Published January, 1984

Recommended for: all duplicate players

ISBN 0-910791-07-4 paperback

Test Your Play As Declarer, Volume 1
by Jeff Rubens and Paul Lukacs
$5.95

Any reader who studies this book carefully will certainly become much more adept at playing out a hand. There are 89 hands here, each emphasizing a particular point in declarer play. The solution to each problem explains how and why a declarer should handle his hands in a certain way. A reprint of the original.

Published December, 1983

Recommended for: intermediate through expert

ISBN 0-910791-12-0 paperback

Devyn Press Book of Partnership Understandings
by Mike Lawrence
$2.95

Stop bidding misunderstandings before they occur with this valuable guide. It covers all the significant points you should discuss with your partner, whether you are forming a new partnership or you have played together for years.

Published December, 1983

Recommended for: novice through expert

ISBN 0-910791-08-2 paperback

101 Bridge Maxims
by H. W. Kelsey
$7.95

The experience of a master player and writer condensed into 101 easy-to-understand adages. Each hand will help you remember these essential rules during the heat of battle.

Published December, 1983

Recommended for: bright beginner through advanced.

ISBN 0-910791-10-4 paperback

Play Bridge with Mike Lawrence
by Mike Lawrence
$9.95

Follow Mike through a 2-session matchpoint event at a regional tournament, and learn how to gather information from the auction, the play of the cards and the atmosphere at the table. When to go against the field, compete, make close doubles, and more.

Published December, 1983

Recommended for: bright beginner through expert.

ISBN 0-910791-09-0 paperback

Play These Hands With Me
by Terence Reese
$7.95

Studies 60 hands in minute detail. How to analyze your position and sum up information you have available, with a post-mortem reviewing main points.

Published December, 1983

Recommended for: intermediate through expert.

ISBN 0-910791-11-2 paperback

THE BEST OF DEVYN PRESS
Bridge Books

A collection of the world's premier bridge authors have produced, for your enjoyment, this wide and impressive selection of books.

MATCHPOINTS
by Kit Woolsey
$9.95

The long-awaited second book by the author of the classic *Partnership Defense*. *Matchpoints* examines all of the crucial aspects of duplicate bridge. It is surprising, with the wealth of excellent books on bidding and play, how neglected matchpoint strategy has been—Kit has filled that gap forever with the best book ever written on the subject. The chapters include: general concepts, constructive bidding, competitive bidding, defensive bidding and the play.

Published October, 1982

Recommended for: intermediate through expert.

ISBN 0-910791-00-7 paperback

DYNAMIC DEFENSE
by Mike Lawrence
$9.95

One of the top authors of the '80's has produced a superior work in his latest effort. These unique hands offer you an over-the-shoulder look at how a World Champion reasons through the most difficult part of bridge. You will improve your technique as you sit at the table and attempt to find the winning sequence of plays. Each of the 65 problems is thoroughly explained and analyzed in the peerless Lawrence style.

Published October, 1982.

Recommended for: bright beginner through expert.

ISBN 0-910791-01-5 paperback

MODERN IDEAS IN BIDDING
by Dr. George Rosenkranz and Alan Truscott
$9.95

Mexico's top player combines with the bridge editor of the <u>New York Times</u> to produce a winner's guide to bidding theory. Constructive bidding, slams, pre-emptive bidding, competitive problems, overcalls and many other valuable concepts are covered in depth. Increase your accuracy with the proven methods which have won numerous National titles and have been adopted by a diverse group of champions.

Published October, 1982

Recommended for: intermediate through expert.

ISBN 0-910791-02-3 paperback

THE COMPLETE BOOK OF OPENING LEADS
by Easley Blackwood
$12.95

An impressive combination: the most famous name in bridge has compiled the most comprehensive book ever written on opening leads. Almost every situation imaginable is presented with a wealth of examples from world championship play. Learn to turn your wild guesses into intelligent thrusts at the enemy declarer by using all the available information. Chapters include when to lead long suits, dangerous opening leads, leads against slam contracts, doubling for a lead, when to lead partner's suit, and many others.

Published November, 1982.

Recommended for: beginner through advanced.

ISBN 0-910791-05-8 paperback

 THE BEST OF DEVYN PRESS
Bridge Books

A collection of the world's premier bridge authors have produced, for your enjoyment, this wide and impressive selection of books.

1595

TEST YOUR PLAY AS DECLARER, VOLUME 2
by Jeff Rubens and Paul Lukacs
$5.95

Two celebrated authors have collaborated on 100 challenging and instructive problems which are sure to sharpen your play. Each hand emphasizes a different principle in how declarer should handle his cards. These difficult exercises will enable you to profit from your errors and enjoy learning at the same time.
Published October, 1982.
Recommended for: intermediate through expert.
ISBN 0-910791-03-1 paperback

TABLE TALK
by Jude Goodwin
$5.95

This collection of cartoons is a joy to behold. What Snoopy did for dogs and Garfield did for cats, Sue and her gang does for bridge players. If you want a realistic, humorous view of the clubs and tournaments you attend, this will brighten your day. You'll meet the novices, experts, obnoxious know-it-alls, bridge addicts and other characters who inhabit that fascinating subculture known as the bridge world.
Recommended for: all bridge players.
ISBN 0-910891-04-X paperback

THE CHAMPIONSHIP BRIDGE SERIES

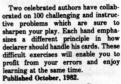

In-depth discussions of the mostly widely used conventions...how to play them, when to use them and how to defend against them. The solution for those costly partnership misunderstandings. Each of these pamphlets is written by one of the world's top experts. **Recommended for: beginner through advanced.**
95 ¢ each, Any 12 for $9.95, All 24 for $17.90

VOLUME I [#1-12] PUBLISHED 1980

1. Popular Conventions by Randy Baron
2. The Blackwood Convention by Easley Blackwood
3. The Stayman Convention by Paul Soloway
4. Jacoby Transfer Bids by Oswald Jacoby
5. Negative Doubles by Alvin Roth
6. Weak Two Bids by Howard Schenken
7. Defense Against Strong Club Openings by Kathy Wei
8. Killing Their No Trump by Ron Andersen
9. Splinter Bids by Andrew Bernstein
10. Michaels' Cue Bid by Mike Passell
11. The Unusual No Trump by Alvin Roth
12. Opening Leads by Robert Ewen

VOLUME II [#13-24] PUBLISHED 1981

13. More Popular Conventions by Randy Baron
14. Major Suit Raises by Oswald Jacoby
15. Swiss Team Tactics by Carol & Tom Sanders
16. Match Point Tactics by Ron Andersen
17. Overcalls by Mike Lawrence
18. Balancing by Mike Lawrence
19. The Weak No Trump by Judi Radin
20. One No Trump Forcing by Alan Sontag
21. Flannery by William Flannery
22. Drury by Kerri Shuman
23. Doubles by Bobby Goldman
24. Opening Preempts by Bob Hamman

THE BEST OF DEVYN PRESS 𝒫

DEVYN PRESS BOOK OF BRIDGE PUZZLES #1, #2, and #3
by Alfred Sheinwold
$4.95 each

Each of the three books in this series is part of the most popular and entertaining collection of bridge problems ever written. They were originally titled "Pocket Books of Bridge Puzzles #1, #2, and #3." The 90 hands in each volume are practical and enjoyable—the kind that you attempt to solve every time you play. They also make perfect gifts for your friends, whether they are inexperienced novices or skilled masters.

Published January, 1981. Paperback

Recommended for: beginner through advanced.

TICKETS TO THE DEVIL
by Ricnard Powell $5.95

This is the most popular bridge novel ever written by the author of Woody Allen's "Bananas," "The Young Philadelphians," and Elvis Presley's "Follow That Dream."

Tickets has a cast of characters ranging from the Kings and Queens of tournament bridge down to the deuces. Among them are:

Ace McKinley, famous bridge columnist who needs a big win to restore his fading reputation.

Carole Clark, who lost a husband because she led a singleton king.

Bubba Worthington, young socialite who seeks the rank of Life Master to prove his virility.

The Dukes and the Ashcrafts, who have partnership troubles in bridge and in bed.

Tony Manuto, who plays for pay, and handles cards as if they were knives.

Powell shuffles these and many other players to deal out comedy, violence and drama in a perfect mixture.

Published 1979. . . Paperback
Recommended for: all bridge players.

PARTNERSHIP DEFENSE
by Kit Woolsey
$8.95

Kit's first book is unanimously considered THE classic defensive text so that you can learn the secrets of the experts. It contains a detailed discussion of attitude, count, and suit-preference signals; leads; matchpoints; defensive conventions; protecting partner; with quizzes and a unique partnership test at the end.

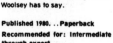

Alan Truscott, Bridge Editor, New York Times: The best new book to appear in 1980 seems certain to be "Partnership Defense in Bridge."

The author has surveyed a complex and vital field that has been largely neglected in the literature of the game. The player of moderate experience is sure to benefit from the wealth of examples and problems dealing with signaling and other matters relating to cooperation in defense.

And experts who feel they have nothing more to learn neglect this book at their peril: The final test of 20 problems has been presented to some of the country's best partnerships, and non has approached a maximum score.

Bridge World Magazine: As a practical guide for tournament players, no defensive book compares with Kit Woolsey's "Partnership Defense in Bridge" which is by far the best book of its kind that we have seen. As a technical work it is superb, and any good player who does not read it will be making one of his biggest errors of bridge judgment.

The author's theme is partnership cooperation. He believes there are many more points to be won through careful play, backed by relatively complete understandings, than through spectacular coups or even through choices among sensible conventions. We agree. If you don't, you will very likely change your mind (or at least modify the strength of your opinion) after reading what Woolsey has to say.

Published 1980. . . Paperback
Recommended for: Intermediate through expert.

DO YOU KNOW YOUR PARTNER? by Andy Bernstein and Randy Baron $1.95 A fun-filled quiz to allow you to really get to know your partner. Some questions concern bridge, some don't — only you can answer and only your partner can score it. An inexpensive way to laugh yourself to a better partnership.

Published 1979   paperback
Recommended for: all bridge players.

DEVYN PRESS
151 Thierman Lane
Louisville, KY 40207
(502) 895-1354

ORDER FORM

VISA AND MASTER
CARD ACCEPTED

**Number
Wanted**

_____	101 BRIDGE MAXIMS, Kelsey.......................... x $7.95 =		
_____	PLAY BRIDGE WITH MIKE LAWRENCE, Lawrence....... x 9.95 =		
_____	PARTNERSHIP UNDERSTANDINGS, Lawrence.......... x 2.95 =		
_____	BRIDGE CONVENTIONS COMPLETE, Kearse.......... x 17.95 =		
_____	PLAY THESE HANDS WITH ME, Reese.................. x 7.95 =		
_____	TEST YOUR PLAY AS DECLARER, VOL. 1, Rubens-Lukacs x 5.95 =		
_____	MATCHPOINTS, Woolsey...................................... x 9.95 =		
_____	DYNAMIC DEFENSE, Lawrence .... x 9.95 =		
_____	MODERN IDEAS IN BIDDING, Rosenkranz-Truscott .... x 9.95 =		
_____	COMPLETE BOOK OF OPENING LEADS, Blackwood .... x 12.95 =		
_____	TEST YOUR PLAY AS DECLARER, VOLUME 2, Rubens-Lukacs . x 5.95 =		
_____	TABLE TALK, Goodwin .... x 5.95 =		
_____	PARTNERSHIP DEFENSE, Woolsey .... x 8.95 =		
_____	DEVYN PRESS BOOK OF BRIDGE PUZZLES #1, Sheinwold ..... x 4.95 =		
_____	DEVYN PRESS BOOK OF BRIDGE PUZZLES #2, Sheinwold ..... x 4.95 =		
_____	DEVYN PRESS BOOK OF BRIDGE PUZZLES #3, Sheinwold ..... x 4.95 =		
_____	INDIVIDUAL CHAMPIONSHIP BRIDGE SERIES (Please specify) x .95 =		
_____	TICKETS TO THE DEVIL, Powell .... x 5.95 =		
_____	DO YOU KNOW YOUR PARTNER?, Bernstein-Baron .... x 1.95 =		

**_QUANTITY DISCOUNT
ON ABOVE ITEMS:_
10% over $25, 20% over $50**

_We accept checks, money
orders and VISA or MASTER
CARD. For charge card
orders, send your card number and expiration date._

SUB TOTAL [_____]

LESS QUANTITY DISCOUNT [_____]

TOTAL [_____]

_____ THE CHAMPIONSHIP BRIDGE SERIES
VOLUME 1.................................... x $9.95 (No further discount) [_____]

_____ THE CHAMPIONSHIP BRIDGE SERIES
VOLUME II .... x 9.95 (No further discount) [_____]

_____ ALL 24 OF THE CHAMPIONSHIP
BRIDGE SERIES .... x 17.90 (No further discount) [_____]

ADD SHIPPING:
  60¢ for 1 ITEM   TOTAL FOR BOOKS [_____]
  $1.00 FOR 2 ITEMS OR MORE   SHIPPING ALLOWANCE [_____]
  SHIP TO: AMOUNT ENCLOSED [_____]

NAME_____

ADDRESS_____

CITY_____STATE_____ZIP _____